BEADS TO BUCKSKINS

BY
PEGGY SUE HENRY

Beading Patterns and Designs of the Native North American Indian
with Illustrated and Written Instructions

Contents

Introduction

Indian beadwork is a rare and exquisite art passed down through centuries of time. Beadworkers of old spent countless hours stringing tiny beads together to form intricate designs.

A great many people believe the native American Indian had very little creative ability and find their art culture primitive with no thought behind it. Until recently, their art was considered crude, with a low social rank.

The world simply didn't understand the purpose of Indian Art. Their beaded shirts and ornaments reflected their whole life style — sometimes telling stories of long, hard winters and tribal moves, recorded as they moved from one valley to another. Buffalo hunts and kills were frequently portrayed on war shields and special ponies trained for hunting buffalo were painted to signify speed and bravery.

Births, deaths and, sometimes, destruction of complete tribes due to some tragedy were recorded on animal skins. Location of certain sacred sites and personal family records, as well as their accomplishments, were worn on their garments. Sometimes, happy stories — with their stick-like figures for the children to enjoy — were recorded on animal skins. It isn't necessary to create an exact likeness to understand the subject. Today's contemporary artists are much more extreme and their work is understood at a glance by many.

Before the white man came to the North American Continent, the native Indian women dyed seeds and various pieces of wood and porcupine quills to use as decoration on robes and garments and other articles, such as belts, moccasins, warbonnets, leggins, pouches, hairpieces, cradle boards, knife sheaths and necklaces. Animal teeth, shells and certain bones were highly prized. The quillwork is said to have been done only in North America and no where else.

With the arrival of the white man came the glass bead. (I understand that Manhattan Island was traded for about 24 pounds of glass beads.) The Hudson Bay Co. traded blankets and glass beads for fur pelts. The trading of beads progressed very quickly to the Plains Indians and the West Coast tribes.

Just as the automobile replaced the horse and wagon in their modern age, gold and silver coins and paper monies have replaced glass beads. Glass beads are no longer considered as something of great value. Yet, when they are placed on an evening dress or costume, the garment becomes very expensive; and if you are lucky enough to purchase some original, old glass beads, then your garment becomes even more expensive. A single antique bead — two or three hundred years old — may be very valuable.

The beautiful, bright-colored glass beadwork done 200 years ago are today highly prized and sought after. Some are very valuable, and even the wornout moccasins with beadwork still attached are collected.

Several years ago, as a child, I remember traveling through New Mexico and Arizona and seeing Navajo women sitting on the ground in front of little lean-tos along the highway weaving beautiful rugs on their centuries-old looms. That same rug that was purchased for five or ten dollars then is valued now at one hundred to thousands of dollars, depending on style, condition and, of course, workmanship.

My Navajo mother (adopted) has enlightened me to the talented people on the Navajo reservation. The basket weavers create elaborate baskets with designs and patterns second to none in the world. Again, these are very sought after and expensive. Then there were the pottery makers who made their geometrical paintings of animal scenes and dancers in full ceremonial dress fired onto their pottery.

All of this type of Indian art is given a great deal of thought and planning beforehand. Most native American art work was done on items used everyday. The women took great pride in decorating their dwellings and clothing, just as the modern women of today do. The archeologists delight in discovering pottery or skins with a bit of history recorded on them.

My whole purpose in writing this book is to help expose and teach a part of this wonderful culture and art that could very quickly disappear from this modern world. There is a saying among the Indians, *"Those that learn nothing from the past, must relive it."* We must learn from the past and incorporate it with today's culture and in this way nothing can be lost.

In the following pages you will find patterns, along with illustrated and written instructions, on how to do many different beading techniques.

About the Author

For several years, people, both Indian and Anglo, have asked me to teach them to do beadwork. I have protected my techniques and also methods of doing old techniques very selfishly, sharing only what I thought would be copied anyway.

I've always had an overpowering interest in Native American lifestyles, and since I am Native American Indian, a large part of my life has been spent in research, mainly centered on beadwork and garments.

My primary business is making fur and leather garments and authentic costumes. The beadwork is a large part of it. Over 50 percent of all buckskin garments I make call for beads or beadwork of some kind.

Realizing the secrets I'm protecting are part of a culture that could easily disappear unnoticed, I have decided to publish the patterns I have acquired and researched over the years, hoping they will be used and not forgotten.

Represented are not only my own, but many other styles of beadwork done by the Native American Indian nations.

Several books are available on beadwork, but I have yet to find one with the actual patterns along with instructions. I have tried to simplify the instructions schematically and graphically.

It will be impossible to enclose and arrange all my patterns and information in one volume, so I have projected a series of 12 volumes — interjecting how to create authentic buckskin garments and introducing sewing with fur, with information on where to send your skins for tanning, a home tanning method and how to care for them after being put into a garment. Bead making techniques, and how, where and why they were traded will also be included.

Hopefully, this series will be accepted as my small contribution in remembering the Native American Indian.

Acknowledgments

No. 1 ... Photography: Scott Ball, Prescott, AZ, and Sheral Keller, WaKeeney, KS.

No. 2 ... All beadwork shown in this book belongs to author.

No. 3 ... Most patterns and designs shown have been handed down for generations. Their original creator is unknown. Some have been transposed from worn pieces of paper or beadwork. You will find a lot of the Navajo geometric designs which are still used in the rugs they weave today.

No. 4 ... Research ... A special "thanks" to my husband, Richard Henry, for his support and help in researching. Also, my adopted Navajo mother, Heneretta Bedonie, of Flagstaff, AZ.

No. 5 ... Illustrations were done by author.

Jayhawk Rock and Fur Shop
P.O. Box 296
Hill City, KS 67642

Phone: (913) 674-2333

CONTACT THE ABOVE ADDRESS FOR:

1 ... General information on where to purchase beads and beading material.

2 ... Wooden loom used in illustration of this book may be purchased from the above store.

3 ... Merchandisers wishing to purchase this book for resale.

4 ... Individuals wishing to purchase single book, C.O.D.

5 ... Beading leather may be purchased from above store.

Important Notes

No. 1 ... Since this is not a transfer pattern book, it will be necessary to trace the floral pattern you choose to use. Then, spot glue or tack with needle and thread onto a piece of felt or soft leather. Sew through both the tracing paper and felt — the tracing paper next to beads. This keeps the pattern in full view and you never have to guess where to put your needle next.

No. 2 ... Placing the pattern and felt into an embroidery hoop (according to the size of project) will help keep the right amount of stress on the material and the stitches straight, while at the same time keeping the pattern from wrinkling.

No. 3 ... Each pattern in this book is done by hand, not a computer. I cannot guarantee each pattern will turn out perfectly for you. The size of beads used will also vary the pattern some. If using a small bead on the square graph patterns, I suggest you use two (2) beads per square.

No. 4 ... *Never use cotton thread for beading.* It breaks easily and will not hold up. Glass beads sometimes have a sharp edge and will fray the thread. Beading thread is designed to hold up longer and will not fray as much.

No. 5 ... When attaching beadwork to leather, always remember that the leather needle is a small knife and will cut the threads. *Never pass a leather needle through the beads of a finished piece of beadwork.* It will cut all the threads.

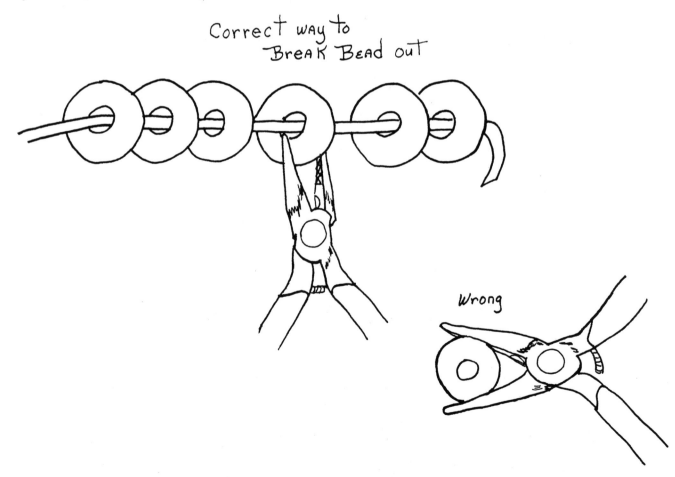

Correct way to Break Bead out

Wrong

Beaded Eagle, 16" across
(background in process of being beaded)

Beaded Gloves

Beaded Necklaces

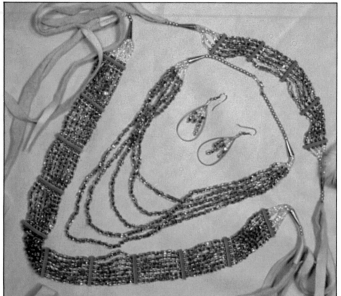

Beaded Accessories

Belt Buckles and Knife Sheath

Beaded Barrettes

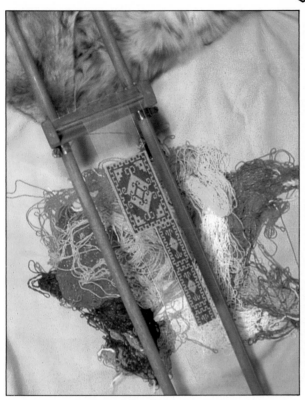

Loom Work in Process

Loom Beaded Strips and Bracelets

Loom Beaded Objects

Loom Beaded Strips

Hair Ornaments

Earrings and Accessories

Earrings

Brick Stitch Earrings

Necklace and Earrings

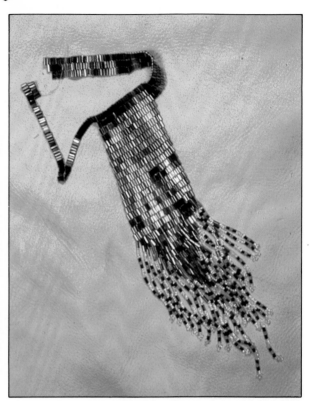

Necklace

Necklace

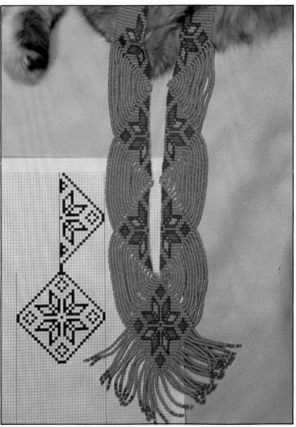

Necklace with Geometric Pattern

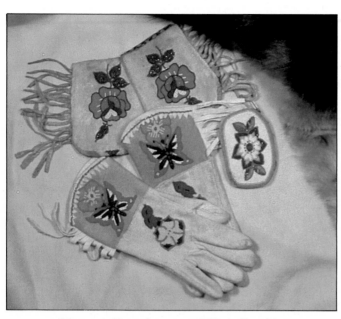

Gloves, Pouches, and Belt Buckle

Beaded Necktie

Beaded Medicine Pouch (front)

Beaded Medicine Pouch (back)

Purse

Purse

Vest

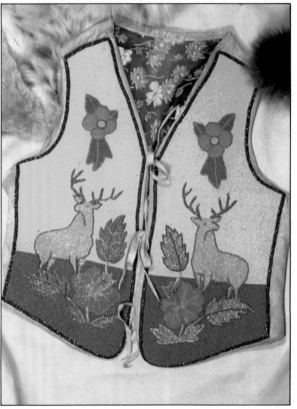

Vest

Moccasins and Hair Piece

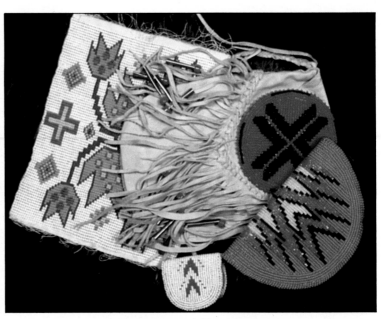

Purse and Pouches

Leggins and Moccasins

Moccasins

Loom Beading

Beading on the loom was one of the more popular techniques used by the North American Indian in the last half of the nineteenth century. The East Coast and Plains Indian favored this method, along with the Lazy Stitch and Overlay Stitch.

Frequently, they used the loom method for armbands, headpieces, strips for leggins, and vests. The women were vibrantly colorful in their beaded buckskin dresses and loomed bead strips around the moccasins. The baby cradle boards were exceptional show pieces. The Medicine Man had certain animals incorporated into his ceremonial dress beadwork, such as turtles, horses, bears, wolves, deer, eagles, and hawks.

Many beautiful loom beaded belts were worn by the Northeastern American Indian as well as the white man that traded with them. The belts were sometimes referred to as wampam belts, when incorporated with seashells.

Loom beading is fun for children. Young people often use it in the scout crafts and school projects, particularly because they can make their own loom from a piece of wood and small nails or screws. Door springs, combs and all sorts of devises can be used to separate the warp threads. The warp threads are the threads placed stationary on the loom. In most pieces, they represent the length of the beadwork project, although loom work can also be square. The warp threads must be placed wide enough apart that the bead fits between each thread.

The loom has been designed many different ways in the past, but I find the design illustrated in Fig. 1 to be the most comfortable one to work with. It is also

possible to make the beadwork as long or

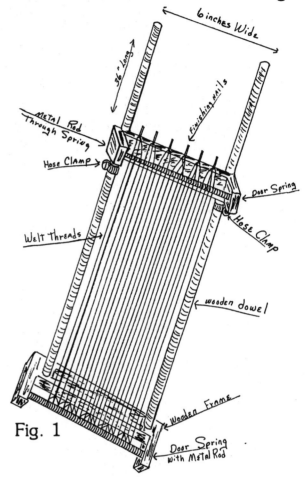

Fig. 1

as short and as wide as you want. When I do belts, I don't have to piece them together from smaller pieces of loomed work for this loom can be let out as long as 36". I can do many dozen pairs of barrettes for the hair without restringing the loom, or two beaded strips side by side at the same time. Split necklaces can be done easily on this loom.

To extend the length of the loom, you simply loosen the hose clamps and slide the top of the loom up on the wooden dowels. Then, retighten the hose clamps firmly and you can begin stringing the warp threads onto the loom.

When I use seed beads on a loom, I space the warp threads in each turn of the spring and always string double threads on the outside edges. This gives the edges of the beadwork a little more strength since these areas catch more wear most of the time. The warp strings should not have any slack; they should be very taut. If you don't wish to construct this loom, it can be purchased. You will find the purchasing address on Page 7 of this book.

To begin stringing the loom, you must tie the thread onto the outside nail, depending on how wide you wish to bead your strip. If it is an inch-wide strip, use the center of the loom. If you are using 12 beads wide, you will need to string 13 strings, then double the outside edge strings as illustrated in Fig. 2. Keep the string tightly drawn, allowing no slack while stringing. I find it easier to keep the slack out if I wrap the string around the nail twice each time before going to the other end of the loom.

After completely stringing the loom, if you find there is too much slack, loosen the hose clamps very carefully — just

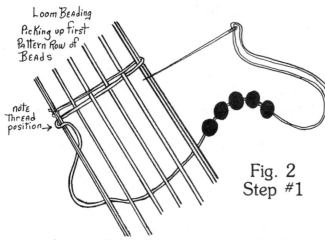

Loom Beading
Picking up first
Pattern Row of
Beads

note
Thread
position →

Fig. 2
Step #1

enough to tightly slide the top of the loom to a tighter position. Hold tightly at all times to prevent the threads from becoming loose and tangled.

If you are using a smaller commercial loom, as illustrated in Fig. 1-A, loosen the wing nut and roll the wooden dowel till string is tightly drawn. Be careful not to bow the wire loom or this will make your finished beadwork too tight and cause it to look wrinkled.

Now you are ready to begin beading. Use only thread designed for beading, not cotton or regular sewing thread. Most hobby shops or complete department stores carry beading threads and needles.

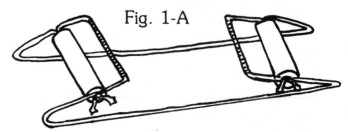

Fig. 1-A

Thread your beading needle with about one yard of thread, using it doubled. Attach to the doubled left outside edge warp threads, tying a firm knot. This thread will be called your welt thread on which the beads will be strung. With your needle, pick up the first row of beads your pattern calls for, going across the pattern from left to right.

From the back side of the warp threads, the beads are placed between the warps and held in place with the forefinger as shown in Fig. 3. Then the welt thread is brought back through the beads on the top side of the warp threads. Be sure your needle stays on the top side of each warp thread as it passes through each bead for this is what holds each bead in place, Fig. 4.

Hold beads in place from bottom side of warp threads

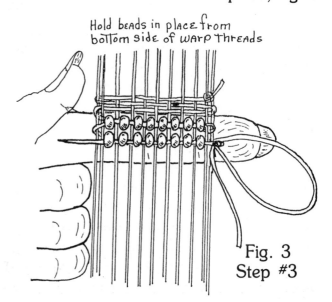

Fig. 3
Step #3

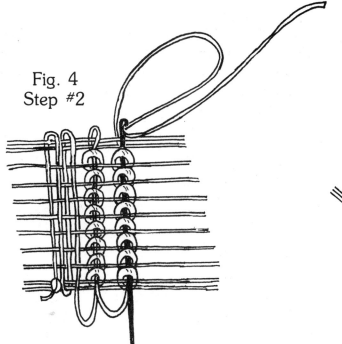

Fig. 4
Step #2

Be sure needle passes through
Top side of warp threads

under between the beading and backing.
If I use the beadwork without backing, I
glue a strip of buckskin or soft leather across
the loose end strings into a fold, as shown
in Fig. 5.

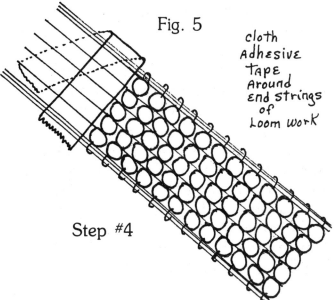

Fig. 5

cloth
Adhesive
Tape
Around
End strings
of
Loom work

Step #4

Always work under good direct light.
It is sometimes difficult to tell the color of
the beads under artificial light, so it's best
to keep the colors separated in small con-
tainers. I find the plastic fish fly tying con-
tainers to be very handy. They stack five
or six high, screw together and are clear
so you may see the colors without open-
ing or labeling each container. (Most
sporting goods stores carry them.)

Beaded strip patterns are not difficult
to do. Once you have become comfortable
with the feel of the loom and familiarize
yourself with the pattern, it goes very fast.
Most patterns repeat themselves within a
few inches on the loom.

A picture is still worth a thousand
words, so I have included a photo of some
of my loom work in process in the color
pages of this book.

The finished bead strip can easily be
sewn onto leather or fabric backing,
depending on your choice. I usually tape
the loose end strips together with cloth tape
or use a little glue and glue them to a small
piece of leather or fabric and tuck them

Loom beaded strips can be used in
combination with other beading techniques
and the finished product is very beautiful
and different, becoming a style of its own
— such as the necklace with geometric
design hanging in the fringe, shown in the
color pages of this book. For several years
I've been asked to reveal my patterns and
techniques on hanging bead fringe. This
particular pattern is one of my favorites.
Although I can't take credit for this design,
I will begin with it.

**Hanging Necklace with Fringe Instruc-
tions:** (This same technique may be used
for any loomed and fringed pattern.)

Step #1:
String the loom for 12 beads wide,
times 13″ long — that will be thirteen (13)
strings on the loom. Be sure to double the
string on the first and thirteenth strings.

Step #2:
Select your beads. For the

background color of this pattern have two full hanks of beads, and for the black edge beads and color combinations, one-half (½) hank each.

Step #3:
Now you may follow the graph pattern on Pages 35, 36, or 37.

The Peyote Stitch

When beading a round object, I find the Peyote Stitch to be the best method. It is used on bolo tie rope necklaces, key chains, earrings, and also covering any object, such as jars, sticks, cigarette lighters, comb handles, purse handles, and metal for bracelets. Its use is unlimited. It can also be made flat.

When I make bolo tie rope, I use a section of cotton clothesline rope for the base and attach the beads to it. If covering a cigarette lighter or key chain or any solid object, first cover the object by sewing leather or felt around it. You may want to spot glue to hold in place while you are sewing (Fig. 1). The pattern depends on the size of project you choose. Small objects require very small beads (size 13.0) for a detailed pattern.

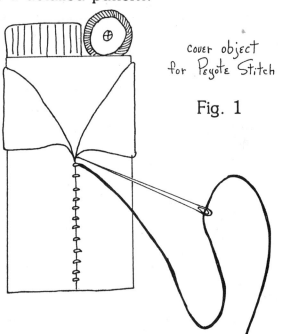

cover object for Peyote Stitch

Fig. 1

Step #1:
Attach knotted thread to object at top of pattern. Pick up three beads of first row of beads going across the pattern. Take a stitch in the leather and bring the needle back through the third bead as illustrated in Fig. 2. (Bringing your needle through the third bead each time you sew three more on keeps the stitches in line and adds

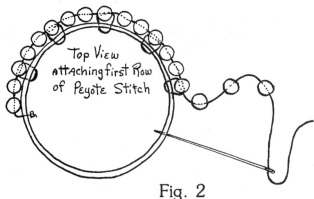

Top View Attaching first Row of Peyote Stitch

Fig. 2

strength to the overall beadwork.) If covering a round object, bring beads around the object, sewing three beads on at a time, using same stitch as above. To connect the circle, pass the needle through the first bead and take a stitch in the leather to strengthen. Be sure that this first row is sewn securely to the leather or felt for it will support the rest of the beadwork.

Step #2 and 3:
Pick up one bead. Bring needle through second bead of first row as illustrated in Step #2. Continue attaching one bead at a time. If going around an object, you don't have to make a turn around at the end of each row — simply

continue around the object until pattern is completed.

Peyote Stitch

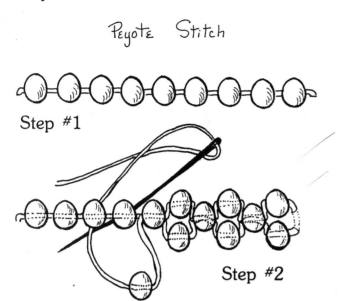

Step #1

Step #2

Step #3

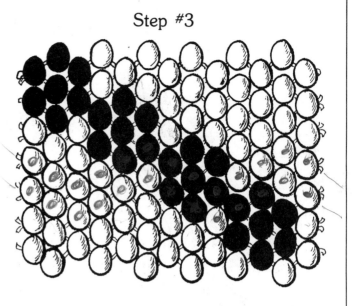

Overlay or Applique Stitch

The Overlay Stitch is sometimes confused with the Lazy Stitch. The finished beadwork appears to be the same, but the technique is different. The Overlay Stitch is an applique method sometimes using two needles. I know it sounds confusing, but actually it's quite simple. Step by step, any of the geometric, animal or floral patterns in this book can be done with the Overlay Stitch.

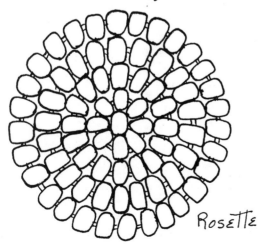

Rosette

Step #1:

To keep your stitches uniform, spot glue or preferably tack with needle and thread a piece of lined notebook paper to a piece of felt. Then place it in an embroidery hoop according to the size of your project.

Step #2:

Thread two beading needles. Work from left to right with geometric patterns. Tie a firm knot in the end of thread; leave knot on the back side of felt. With lined paper on top and using lines vertically, pick up the first row of beads the pattern calls for with your needle. Lay strung beads across the vertical lines on the paper. When beads are straight, take a stitch to the back side of the felt, Fig. 1. Make five rows

Fig. 1

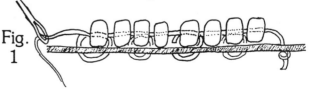

across, following each pattern row. With second needle, stitch down the vertical lines of the notebook paper, as illustrated in Fig. 2.

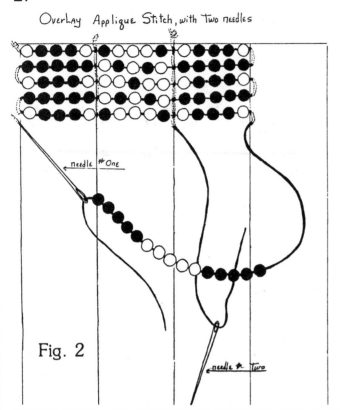

Overlay Applique Stitch, with Two needles

needle #One

needle # Two

Fig. 2

Step #3:

When pattern is complete, remove from hoop and trim felt about ½-inch from beadwork. Tuck felt under, stitching with needle and thread to hold.

Step #4:

Round rosette Overlay Stitch is illustrated in Fig. 3.

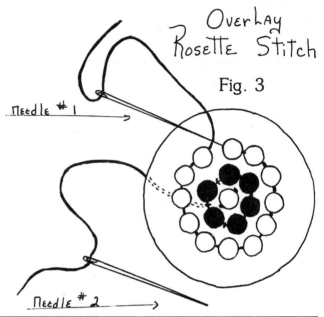

Overlay Rosette Stitch

Fig. 3

Needle #1

Needle #2

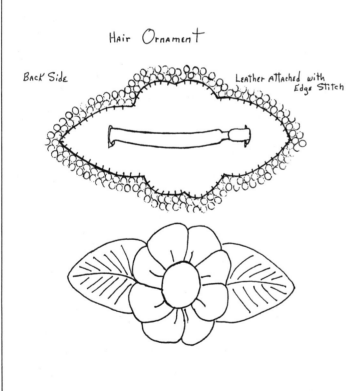

Hair Ornament

Back Side

Leather Attached with Edge Stitch

Beginning Row · 53 Beads

The Lazy Stitch

The Sioux, Cheyenne and Arapaho Indians were well known for their use of the Lazy Stitch. After completing a project using this technique, you will want to rename it — by no means will you consider yourself lazy! It is very rewarding to behold your own accomplished beadwork. It is also easy to get caught up into wanting to do more. We beaders call this, "Bead Fever." Like a good book, you don't want to put it down. And it is a good way to relax and take your mind off everyday pressures.

The Lazy Stitch is a quick method of covering a lot of area in the shortest period of time. As many as eight to ten beads can be sewn on with one stitch, although a tighter and more uniform stitch is usually done with five or six beads. A good Lazy Stitch does not lie flat, but bows just slightly in the middle. This gives the overall beadwork a dimensional and professional look.

Most Lazy Stitch patterns are geometric. In the following pages, I have included easy-to-follow patterns which can be done by the beginner beader as well as the experienced. Many animals are considered difficult to bead. They become very simple when done according to these patterns. The Lazy Stitch is so versatile and can be used in almost any pattern. An eagle, shown in the color pages, is in the process of being beaded freehand-style with no lines and slightly stacked stitches, Fig. 1.

Using a good glass bead is important to any fine work. Good beads mean uniform in size and color. If you are doing a large pattern, be sure you have enough beads when you begin. If you run out of beads during a project and have to buy more, you may have trouble matching the

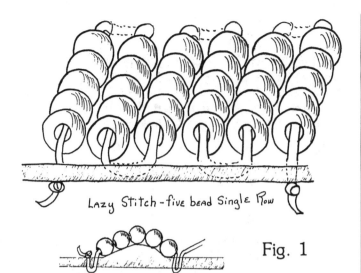

Lazy Stitch - five bead Single Row

Fig. 1

original color. Glass for beads is dyed by lots and the same color will sometimes vary a great deal in shade from one lot to another.

The American Indian covered complete garments, as well as pipe bags, medicine bags, cradle boards, moccasins, leggins, and many other items with the Lazy Stitch. Originally, sinew, made from the dried tendons of an animal, was used as thread for most all beadwork. Today a nylon thread is used. Many old timers still prefer to use sinew to be authentic. I enjoy working with a small size bead, 11-0 to 16-0, so sinew is not practical for any speed at all.

The tightness of the beaded stitch determines how well the beadwork holds and how long it lasts. Loose stitches have a tendency to catch and break the string. I like to lock every other stitch by simply taking an extra stitch in the leather or fabric before picking up the next group of beads on the needle. This prevents losing a lot of beads in case one stitch breaks.

The Lazy Stitch is basically done in straight lines. Rather than draw lines on a piece of felt, I spot glue a piece of lined notebook paper to a piece of felt with

Elmer's® glue, and sew through the paper and the felt at the same time. The combination of paper, glue and felt gives the beadwork the precise firmness for backing, and the paper has perfect lines to follow for precision stitches. Depending on what size bead you choose to work with, five or six beads fit between the vertical lines of the notebook paper perfectly. I usually use the lines vertically (up and down) with each pattern. I suggest size 11-0 beads with six (6) beads to a stitch for the patterns in the following pages.

The Lazy Stitch can be done one or two rows at a time (Fig. 2). For the beginner, I suggest single row (Fig. 1) for the first

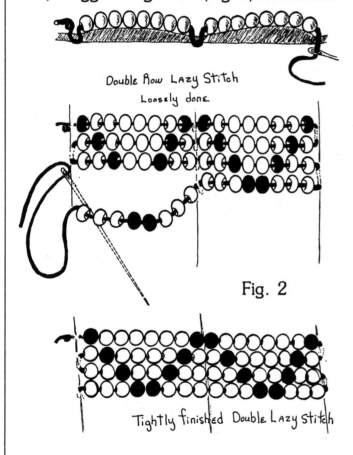

Double Row Lazy Stitch
Loosely done

Fig. 2

Tightly finished Double Lazy Stitch

few rows. Rather than bead directly onto a garment, I prefer to bead on felt or fabric and applique the beadwork to the garment. When the garment wears out or needs cleaning, you can take the beadwork off without damaging it.

Lazy Stitch Instructions

Step #1:
Tie a firm knot in the end of your thread. Leave the knot on the top side of the lined paper and felt (Fig. 2). At the finish of each threading, always tie a firm knot.

Step #2:
Each square in the pattern represents a bead. Pick up six beads on the needle. I begin with the center row of the pattern and work out to each side, row by row.

Step #3:
Trim finished beadwork, leaving about one-half (½)-inch of felt around the whole project. Fold felt to back side of beadwork taking tucks where necessary and spot glue in place.

Step #4:
To protect the stitches on the back side of the beadwork, spot glue a thin piece of leather or felt and stitch around the outside edge. The Edge Stitch is illustrated on Page 25. *(Don't use a lot of glue.)*

Now your beadwork is complete to applique onto anything you wish, or to be worn as jewelry.

Five Edge or Fret Stitching Techniques

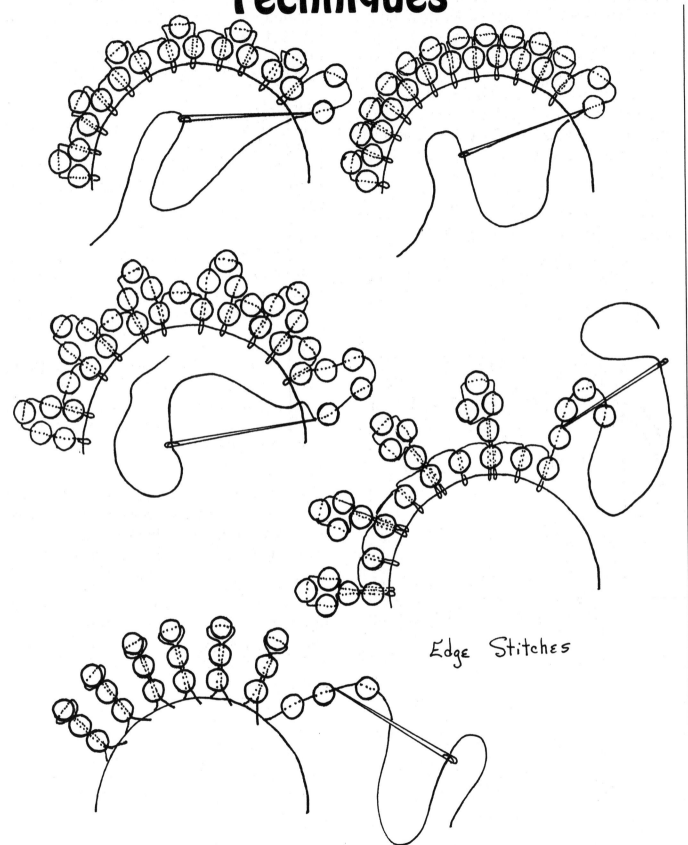

Edge Stitches

25

Loom Beading Without a Loom

o my knowledge, this technique has never been exposed by anyone but the author. I developed this method while traveling in a car years ago on vacation. I forgot to pack my loom and had a special pattern that called for a loomed strip. It's very simple to do and looks better than beadwork actually done on the loom because there are fewer strings showing and no loose-end strings to deal with.

Step #1:

After choosing a pattern, string the full length of beads on the first row going down the pattern. Starting back up the second row, pick up the first two beads of the second row. Attach, as illustrated in Step #1. Continue attaching one bead at a time. When you reach the top of row two, pick up two beads and attach the same as row two. Each time you start a new row, begin with two beads then go to one for the rest of the row.

Step #2:

Certain patterns call for beaded fringe hanging. In order to hang beaded fringe, the hole must be facing down. So do the same stitch as above only sideways — bead across the pattern instead of up and down, as illustrated in Step #2.

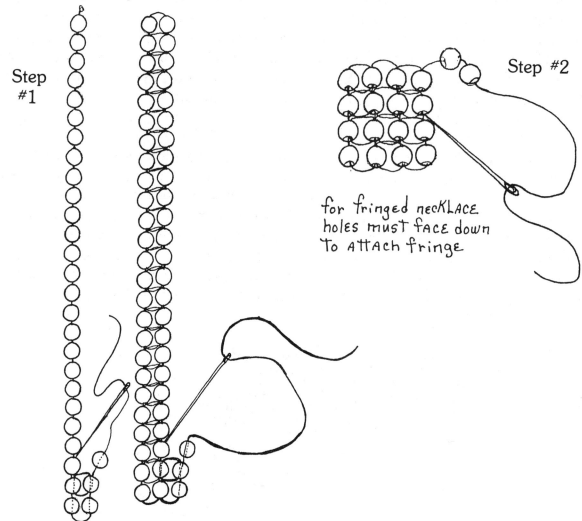

Step #1

Step #2

for fringed neckLAce holes must fAce down To AttAch fringe

The Brick Stitch

The Brick Stitch is complex in appearance, but rather simple to do with a little patience and practice. The author cannot attribute this technique to any certain tribe or nation of North American Indians, although the Pacific Northwest such as Oregon, Washington State, North California, and Idaho Indians have produced some of the finest beadwork using this technique.

The Cheyenne also use it on some of their hair ornaments, bracelets, and moccasins.

The American Indian was well known for trading with other tribes, as well as the Anglo American and Canadian Trading Posts. It's difficult to pinpoint the origin of design. Sometimes the colors of beadwork will reveal much, since many of the tribes were identified by certain colors and their arrangements.

I always enjoy using the Brick Stitch technique on most of the earrings I make because of the variety of designs that can be made. It needs no backing of leather or fabric.

After completing a pair or two of earrings by pattern, you will probably want to design your own. I always get an idea for another pair before the first is finished, so I put my ideas on paper to use as reference for the next project.

Making necklaces with the Brick Stitch can become a lengthy project. So, I suggest the beginner start with a less time-consuming project, such as earrings, to avoid becoming confused and bored before you understand the technique enough to accomplish speed.

The Brick Stitch is an easy and pleasant procedure which will be told to you in simple, clear detail in the pages that follow.

Some of the patterns shown are very old — used by the American Indian for generations — and some are new designs done by the author and modern day Indian and Anglo friends. The step-by-step instructions are illustrated for quick understanding. These patterns and techniques will work for you as they have for the author and others who have had patience enough to try.

For the first pair of earrings, use Bugle beads for the anchor row. You'll find them much easier to work with and can be used for the whole earring if you wish.

If the pattern is followed exactly as illustrated, there should be no threads showing on the finished earring. This is one of the factors that determines an experienced beader from a beginner, and also the value of the beadwork.

Step #1

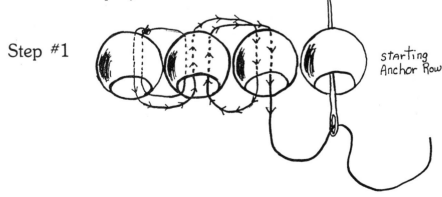

starting Anchor Row

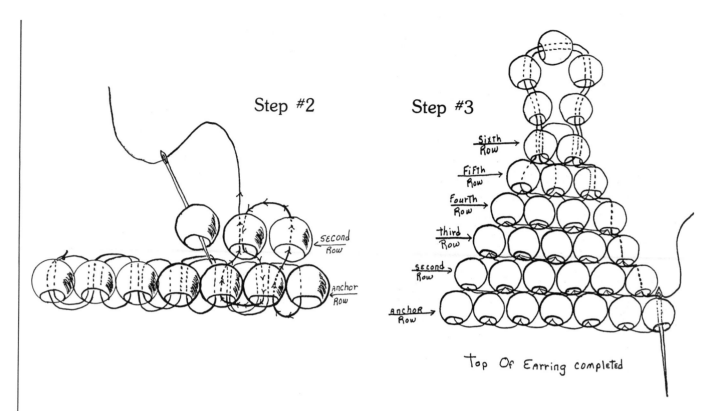

Step #2

Step #3

Second
Row

Anchor
Row

Sixth
Row

Fifth
Row

Fourth
Row

third
Row

Second
Row

Anchor
Row

Top Of Earring completed

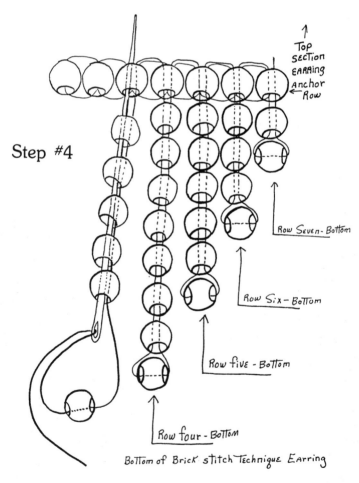

Step #4

Top
Section
Earring
Anchor
Row

Row Seven - Bottom

Row Six - Bottom

Row five - Bottom

Row four - Bottom

Bottom of Brick stitch Technique Earring

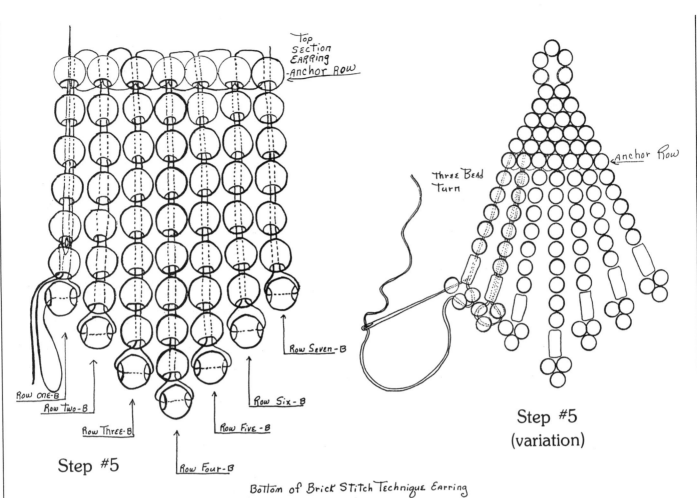

Top
Section
Earring
-Anchor Row

Row Seven-B

Row Six-B

Row Five-B

Row One-B

Row Two-B

Row Three-B

Row Four-B

Step #5

Step #5
(variation)

Three Bead
Turn

Anchor Row

Bottom of Brick Stitch Technique Earring

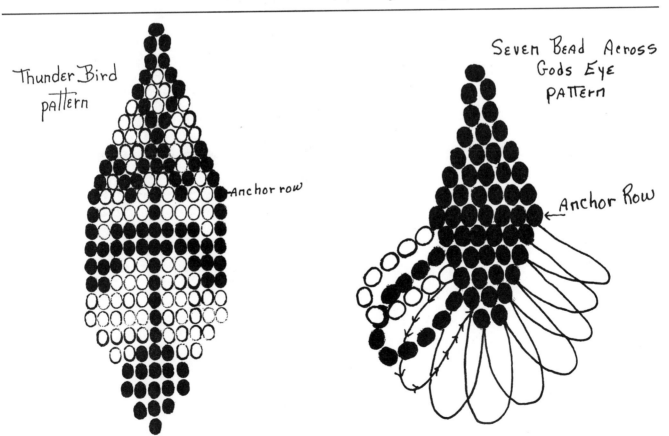

Thunder Bird
pattern

Anchor row

Seven Bead Across
Gods Eye
Pattern

Anchor Row

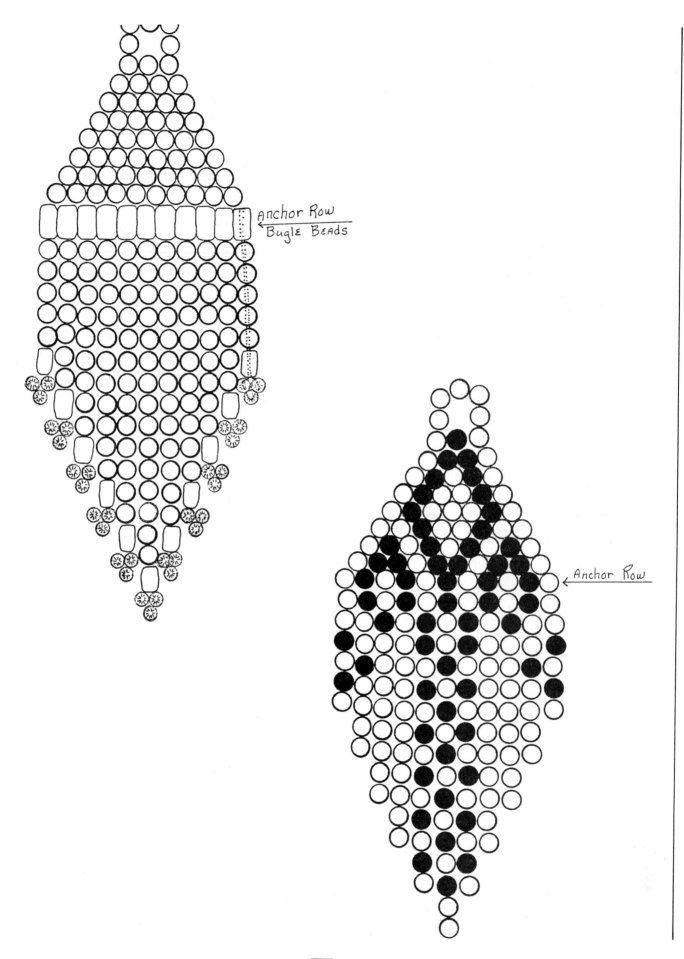

Anchor Row
Bugle Beads

Anchor Row

30

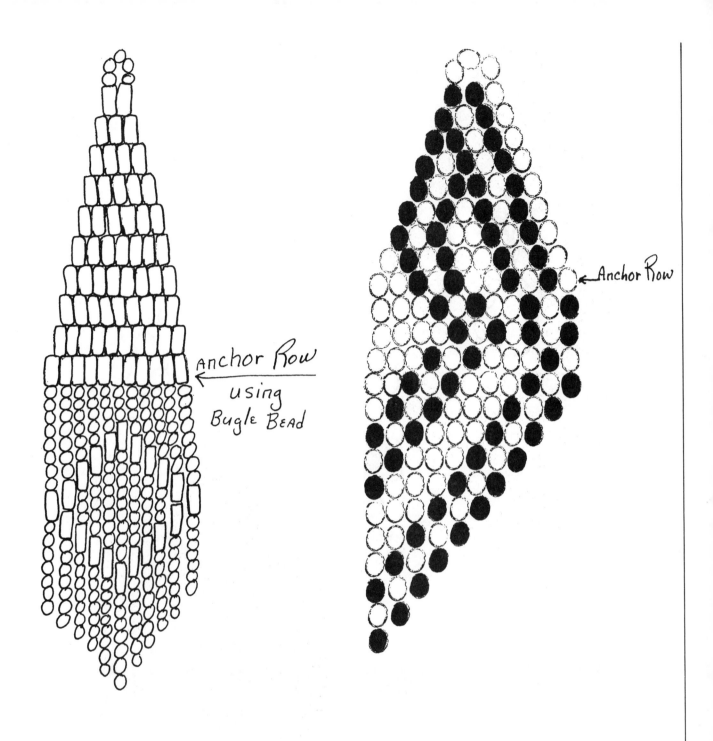

Anchor Row
using
Bugle Bead

Anchor Row

Daisy Chain

The Daisy Chain stitch can be used as a chine on just about any necklace you wish to attach it to. Or, it's a beautiful ornament by itself.

Step #1:
Thread needle with about 25 inches of doubled thread. Pick up five beads with needle on thread. Bring needle through first bead as illustrated in Step #1.

Step #2:
   Pick up two beads; bring needle through fourth bead as illustrated. Continue until you reach the desired length of chain.

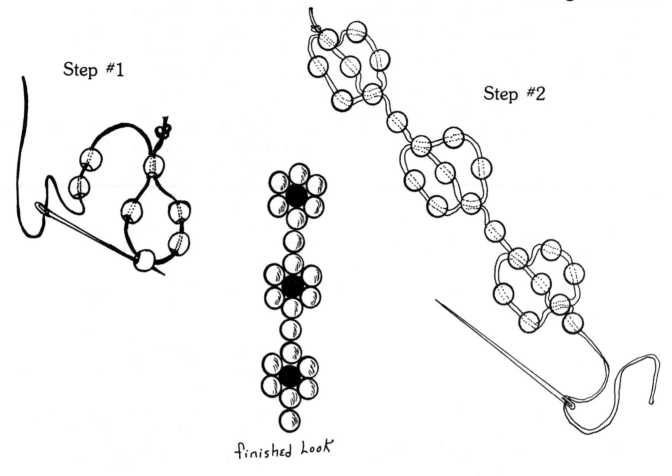

Step #1

Step #2

finished look

Hanging Deer Head Necklace

Arranging glass beads creatively is an art, just as an artist is with a brush and oil paints. Each pattern will reflect your own version — using your choice of colors — making it an original. Inspiration for color design comes with grouping hanks of beads in assorted colors together, then choosing the colors you prefer to work with. It's important to pick a background color you won't grow tired of while doing the pattern. Most beaders work with pastels or white for background — I personally like brighter colors. This deer head necklace shouldn't be attempted as a first project. I suggest something smaller to avoid getting bored until you become adjusted to the feel of the beading needle and acquire a little speed. Should you have too many beads on your thread, you may save time by breaking them out as illustrated on Page 8 (See *Important Notes*.)

Step #1:

This necklace begins with a beaded strip 12 beads wide and 12 inches long, done on the loom. Refer to the loom instructions on Page 17. Use the deer head pattern for the beaded strip.

For the eyes, antler, edge beads, and turn beads on bottom of fringe, I have used a black cut glass bead for accent.

Step #2:

Do not remove the beaded strip from the loom. Holding or laying the loom sideways, do the edge stitch along one side, the full length of the beaded strip, illustrated in Fig. 4.

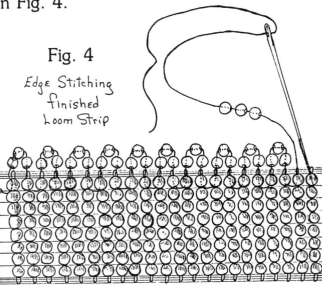

Fig. 4

Edge Stitching
finished
Loom Strip

Step #3:

Find the exact center of the beaded strip. While still on the loom, begin the fringe portion of the necklace. Beginning in the center of your strip, after threading your needle with as long a doubled thread as you feel comfortable with, tie the thread onto the loomed strip.

Hanging Deer Head Necklace

We will work the right half of the deer head first. Refer to the graph pattern. Find center row of fringe on the graphed pattern. With needle, pick up all beads indicated for that fringe row.

Step #4:

Pass needle back through the row of beads, beginning at the bugle bead, leaving six beads for a circle at the bottom of the fringe row. These are called turn beads, Fig. 1.

Step #5:

Work needle through the loomed row indicated for the fringe row you have just completed, Fig. 2. Be sure you don't pull the fringe too tight causing it to hang irregular, thus throwing the pattern off. After achieving the right stress on the fringe, secure it by looping the thread around the edge strings of the loom strip. Should you break a fringe later, this will prevent losing more than one fringe row.

Step #6:

Bring needle down through the next row of loomed beads to the right and repeat Step #5. Continue until right half of deer head is complete. Begin again at the center of beaded strip working to the left. Attach the left side of the deer head fringe.

Step #7:

Before removing beadwork from loom, tape ends of loomed strip with adhesive tape, Fig. 3. Cut loom strings leaving about two inches of the string on each end of beaded strip. Although it isn't necessary, I attach a soft piece of leather to the back side of the loomed strip and use leather ties to connect the necklace. Leather is more comfortable next to the neck and adds a lot of strength to the necklace.

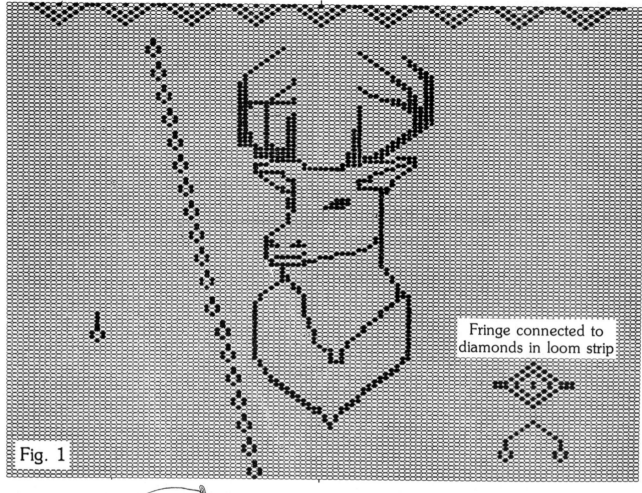

Fig. 1

Fringe connected to diamonds in loom strip

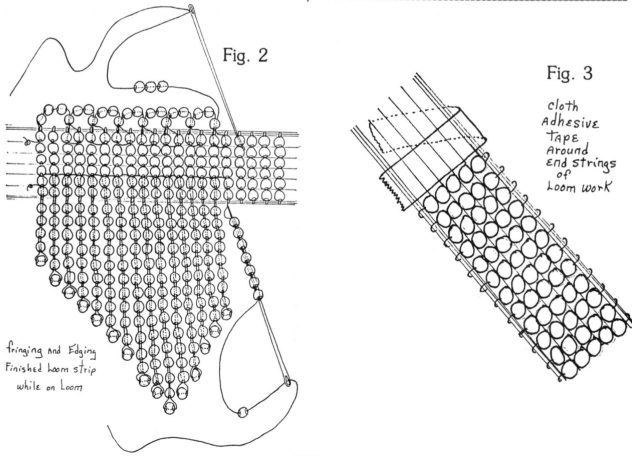

Fig. 2

fringing and Edging
Finished loom strip
while on loom

Fig. 3

cloth
Adhesive
Tape
Around
End strings
of
Loom work

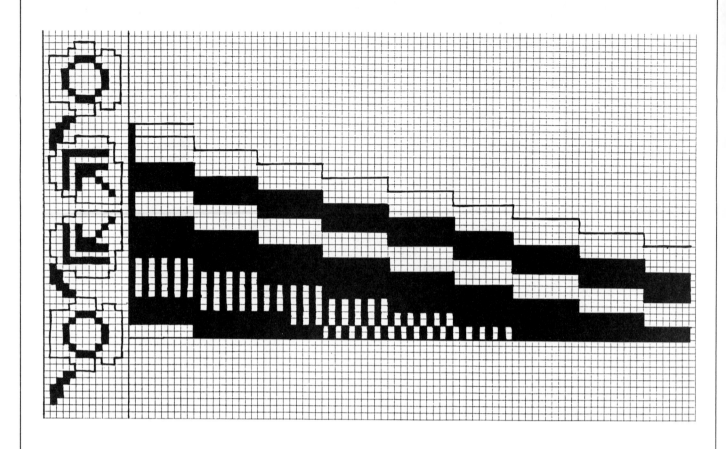

Beaded Loom Strip for Geometric Hanging Necklace
(Also shown in Color Section)

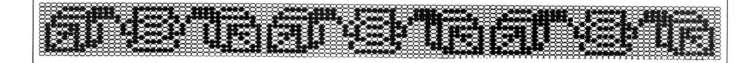

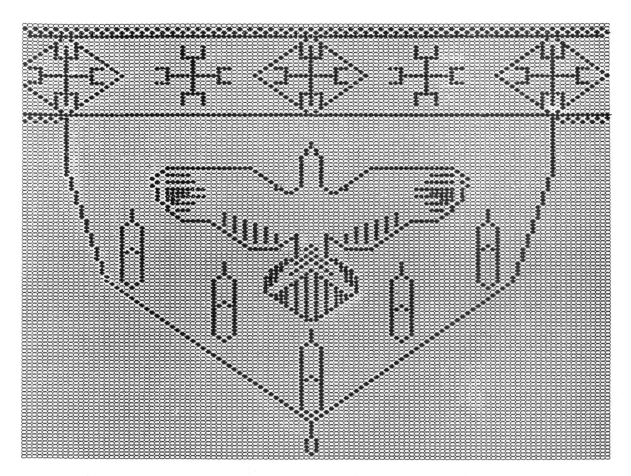

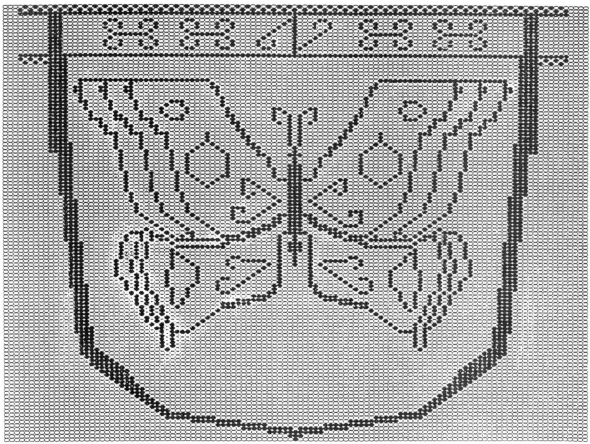

Designs and Patterns
of the Woodland Indian

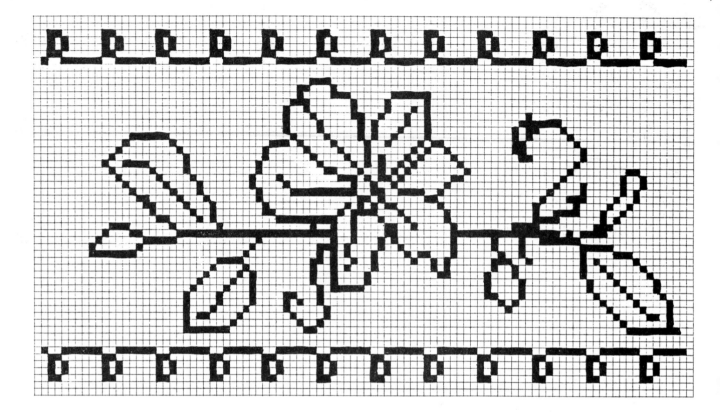

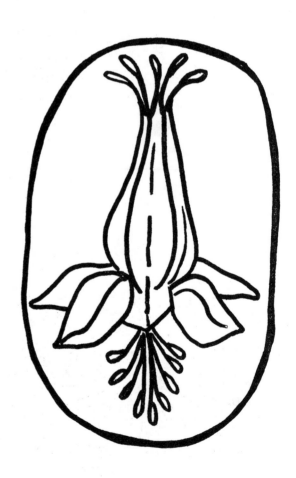

Special Occasion Patterns

Woodland Indian Applique Patterns

floral Pattern for
Woodland Indian Garments and
Hair Ornaments

floral Pattern
for
Woodland Indian Garments

Applique or
Overlay
Stitch
Patterns

Special Occasion Patterns
Bride's, Mothers, Weddings

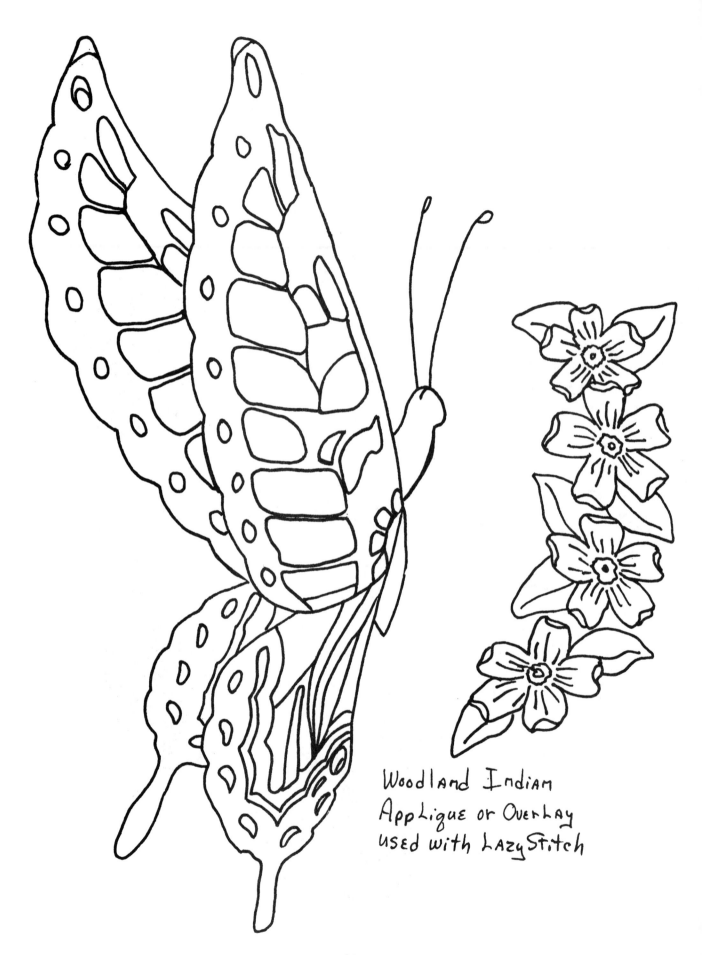

Woodland Indian
Applique or Overlay
used with Lazy Stitch

Woodland
Indian
Overlay or
Lazy Stitch
Pattern

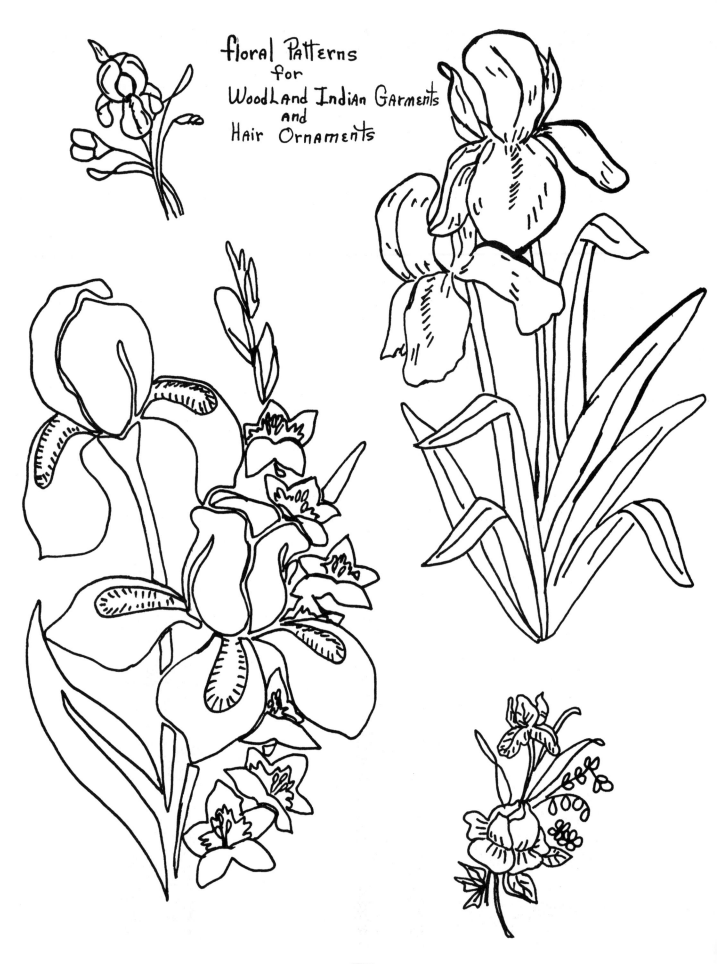

floral Patterns
for
WoodLand Indian Garments
and
Hair Ornaments

Geometric Designs and Patterns

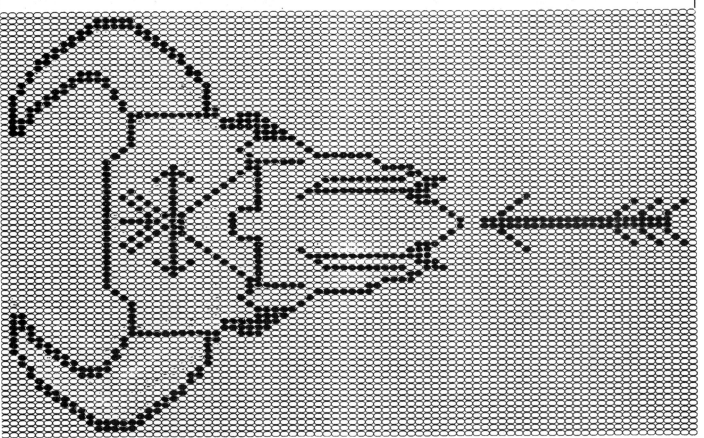

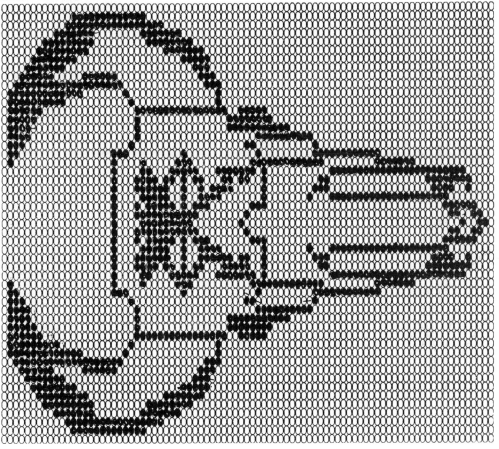

ABCDEFGHIJKLMNO
PQRSTUVWXYZ

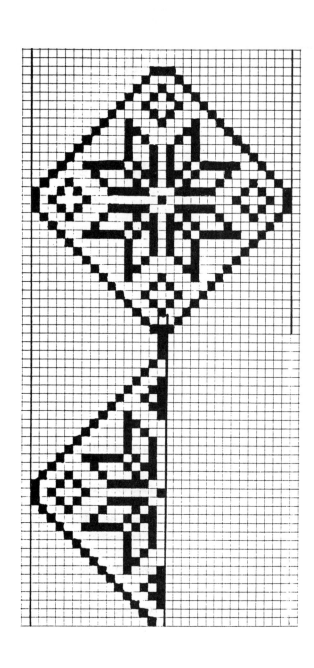

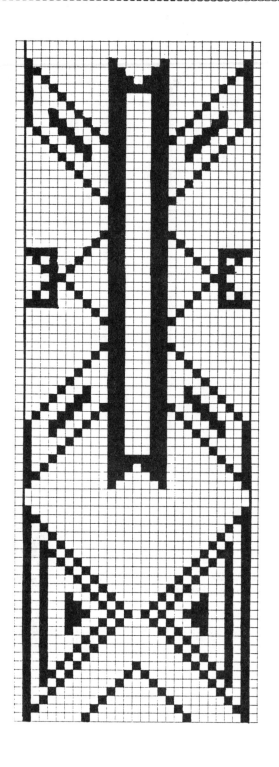

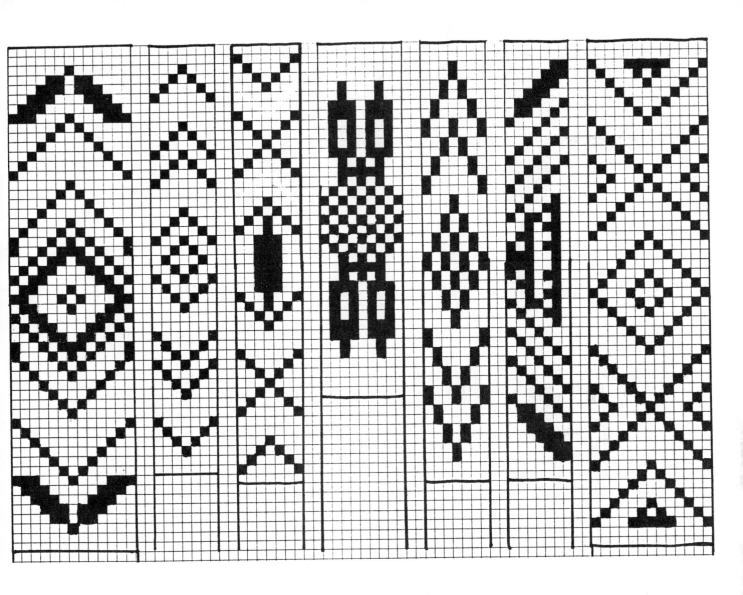

Hair Barrettes Done on Loom
(Also shown in Color Section)

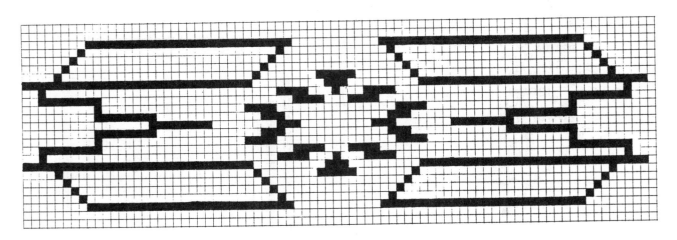

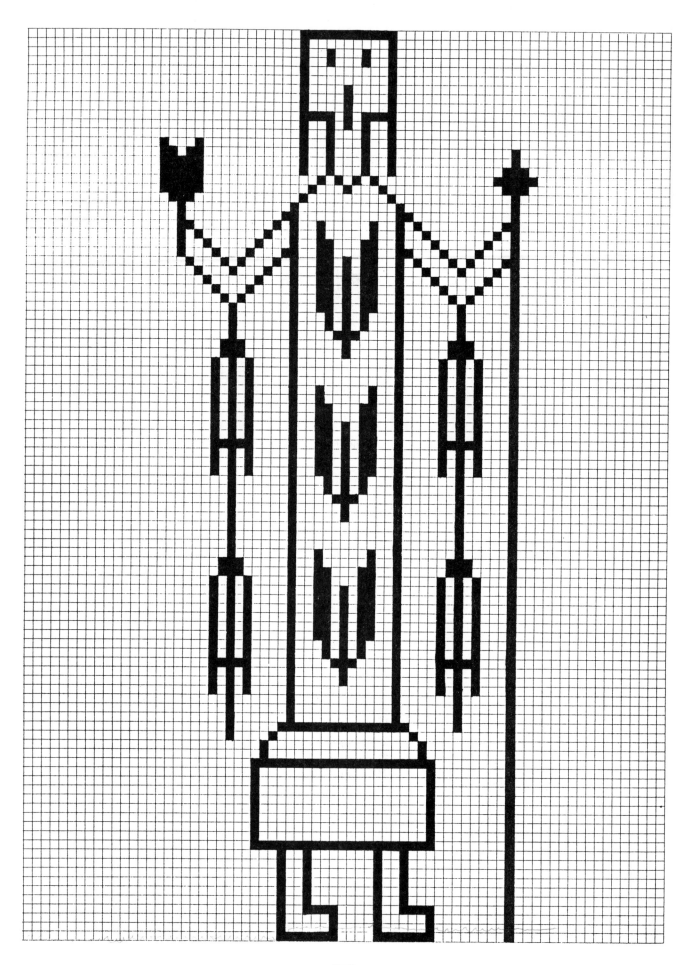

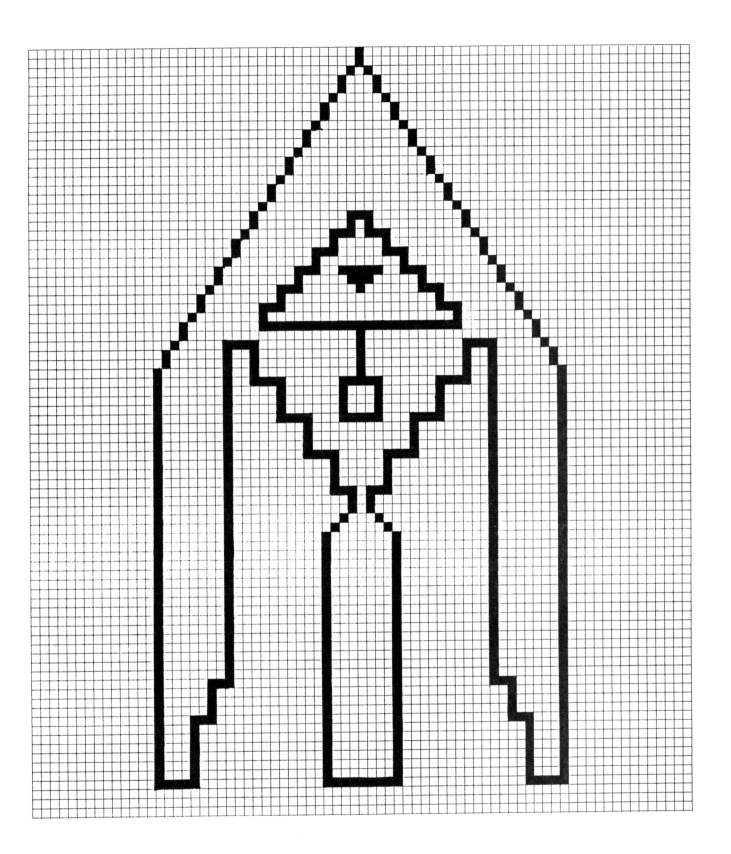

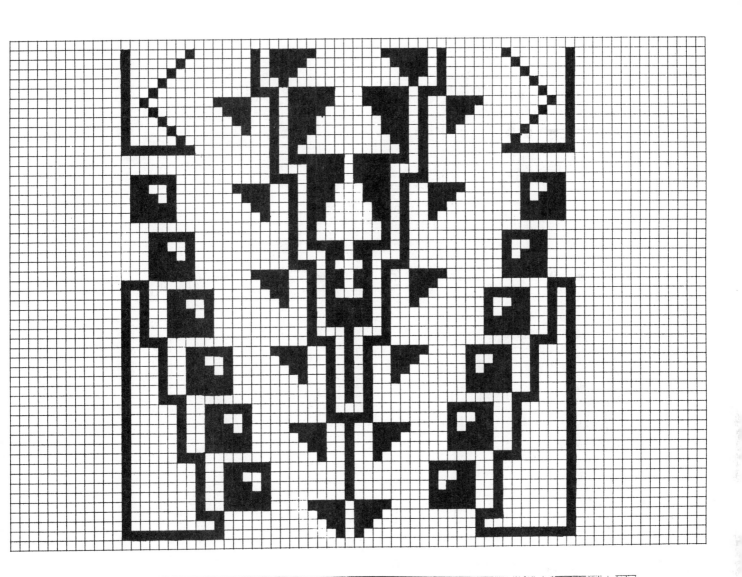

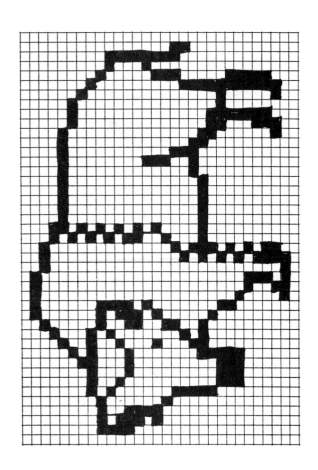

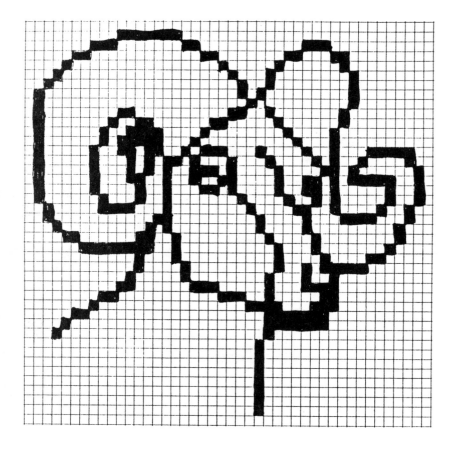

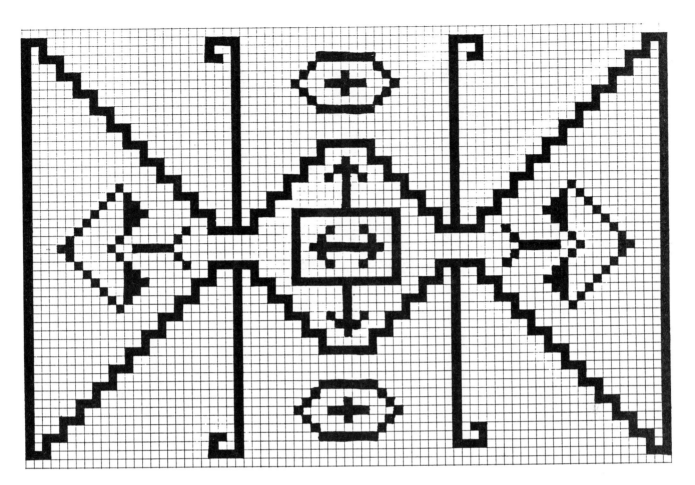

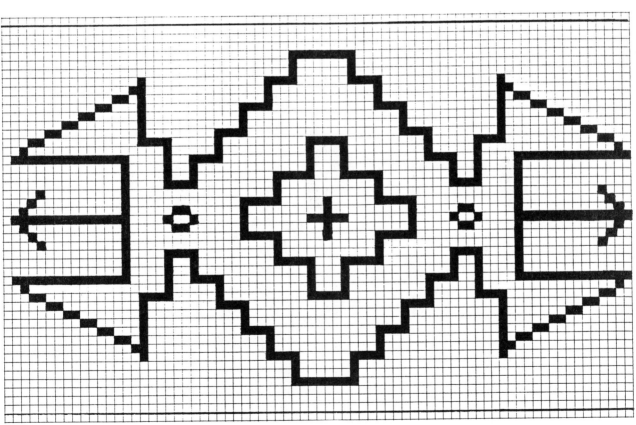

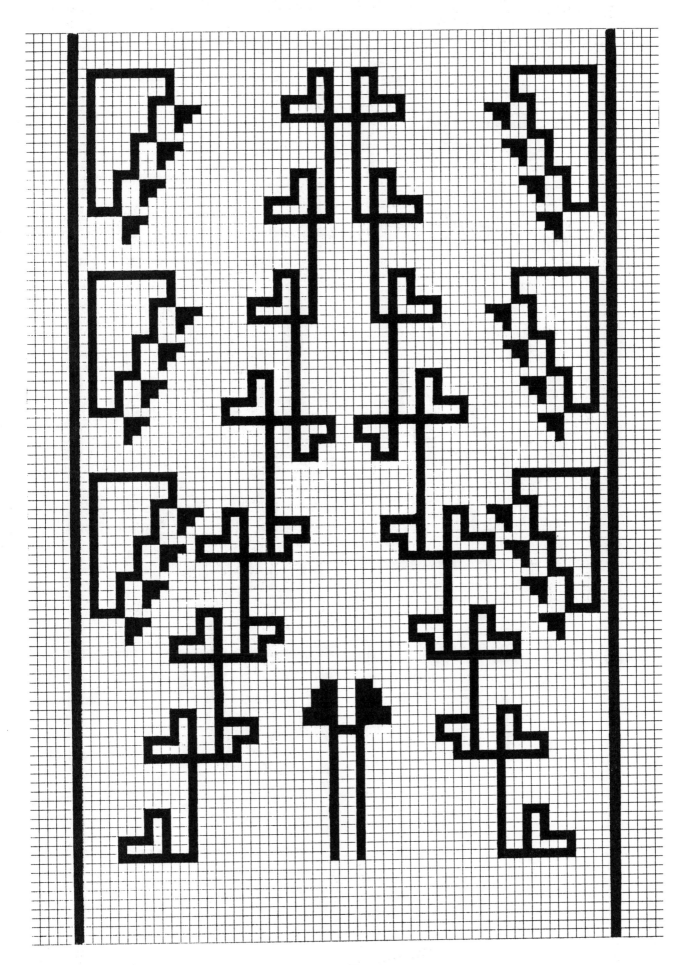

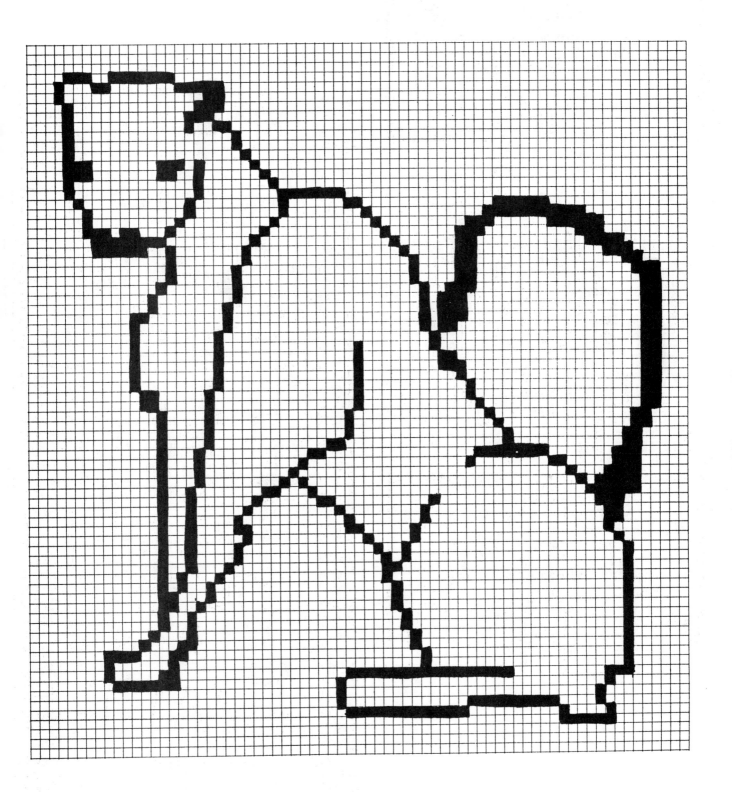

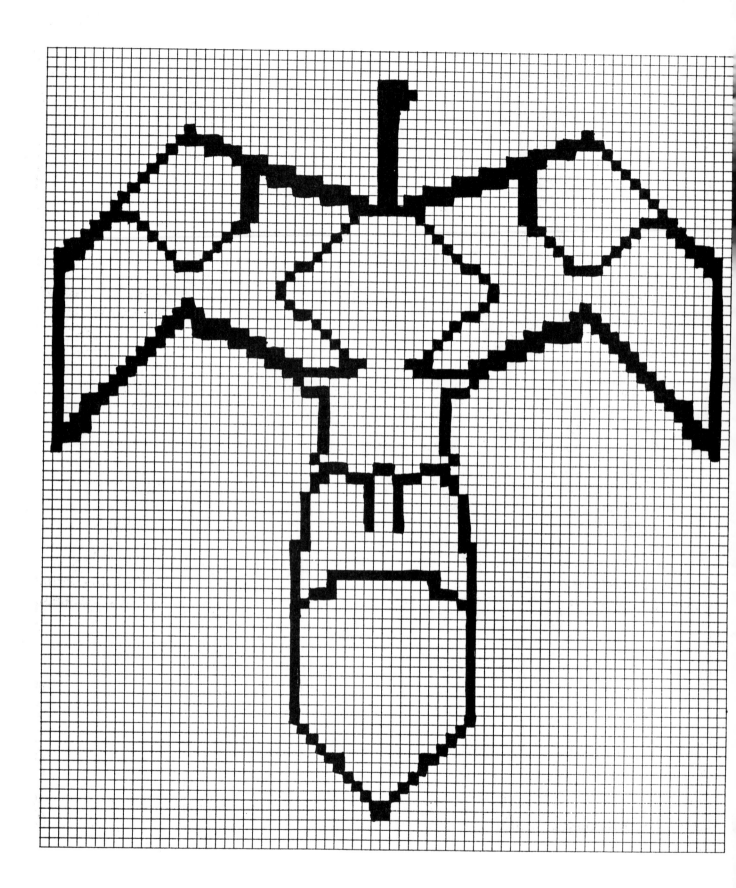

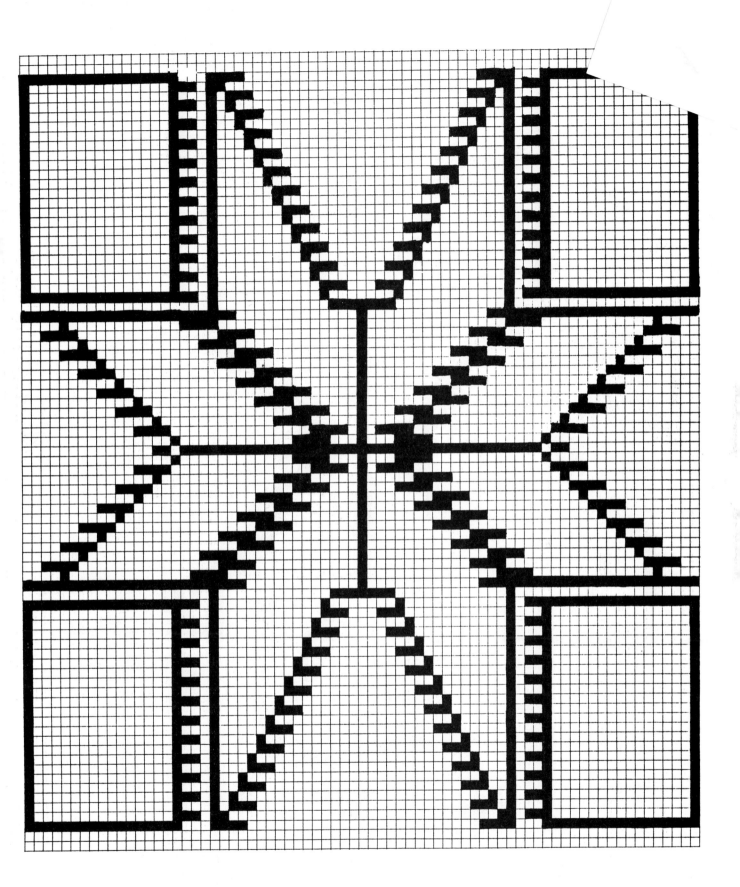

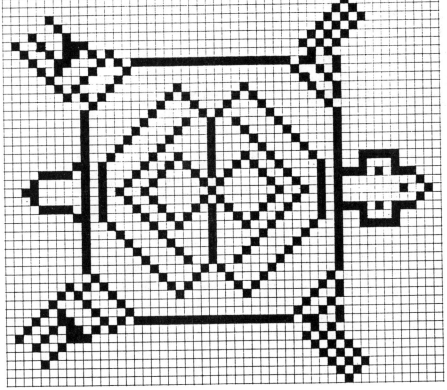

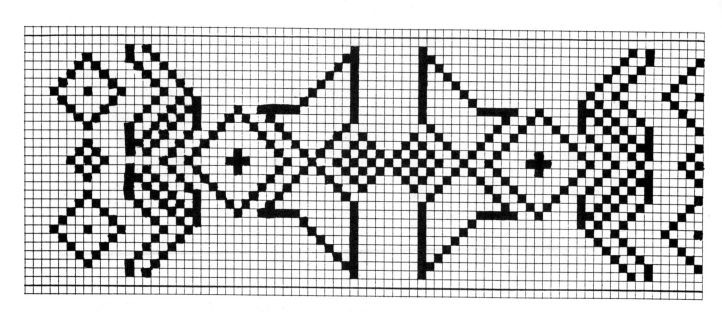

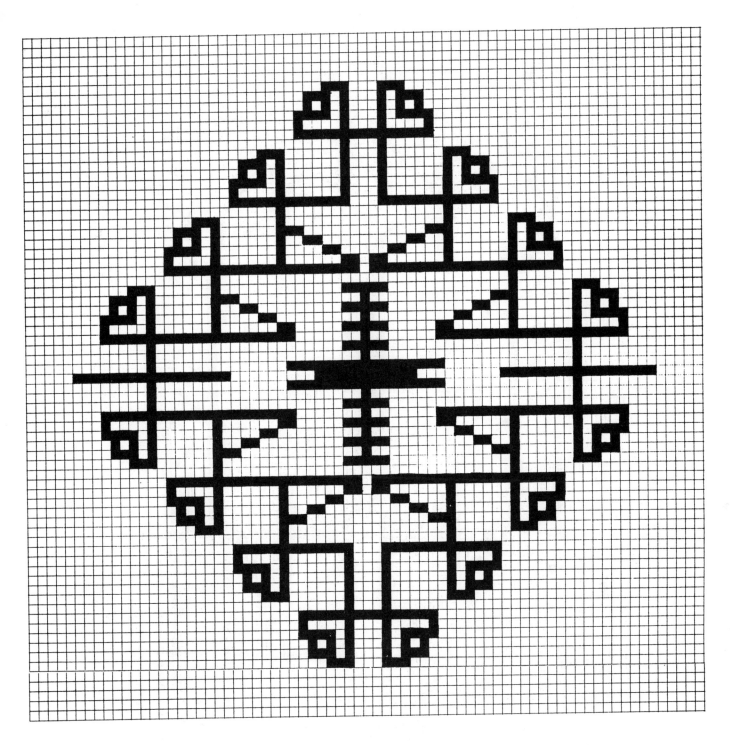

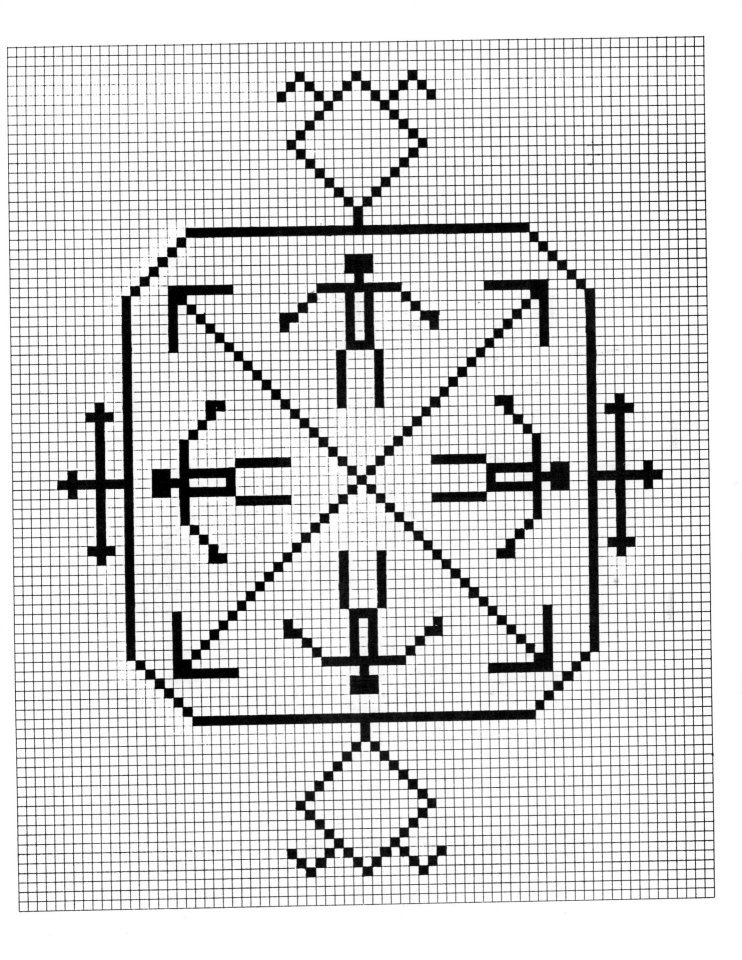

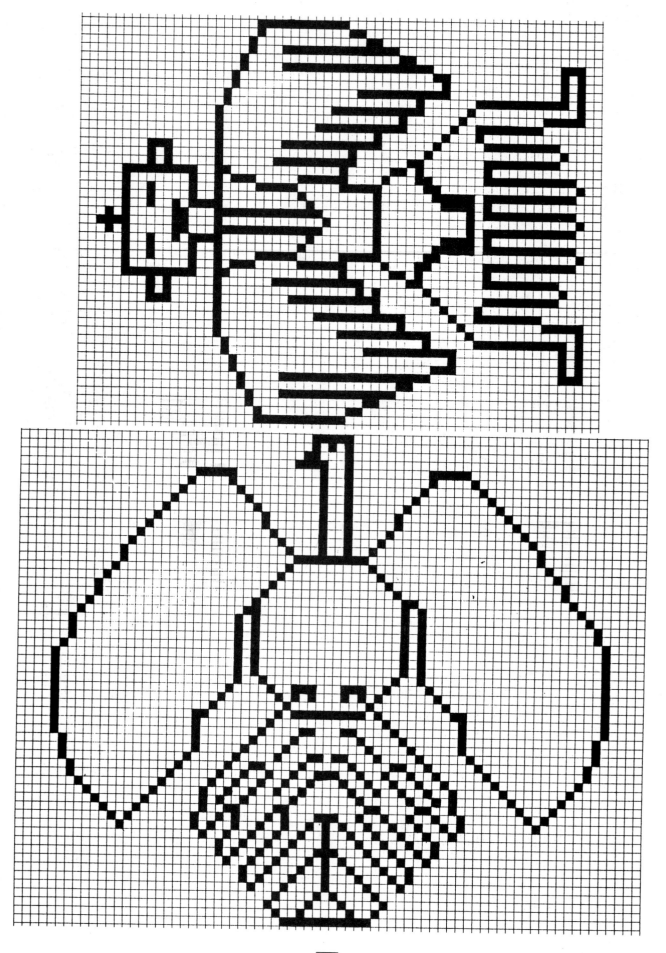

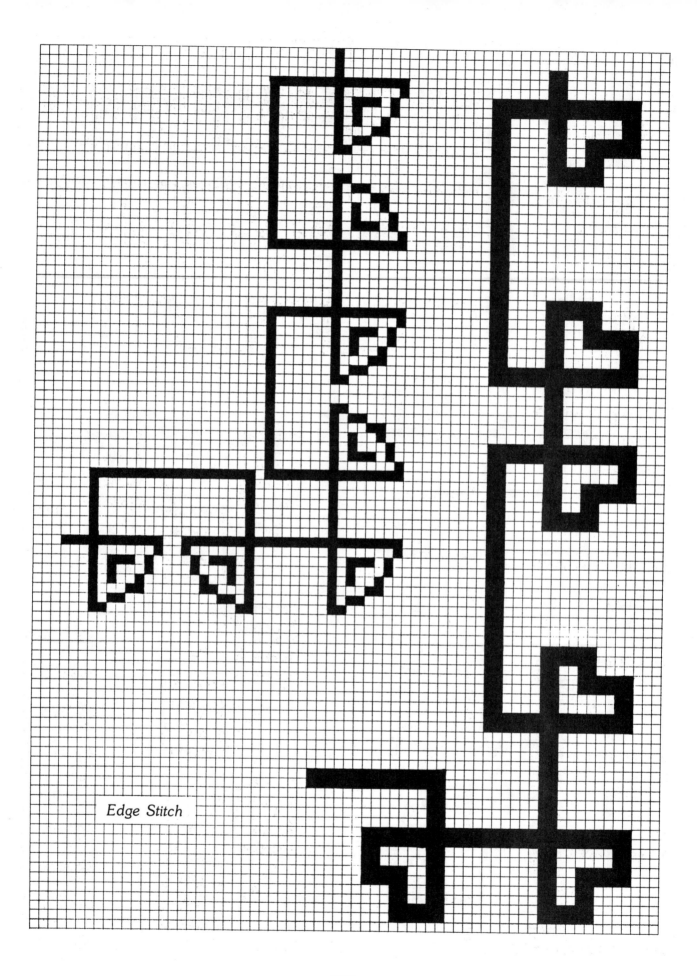

Edge Stitch

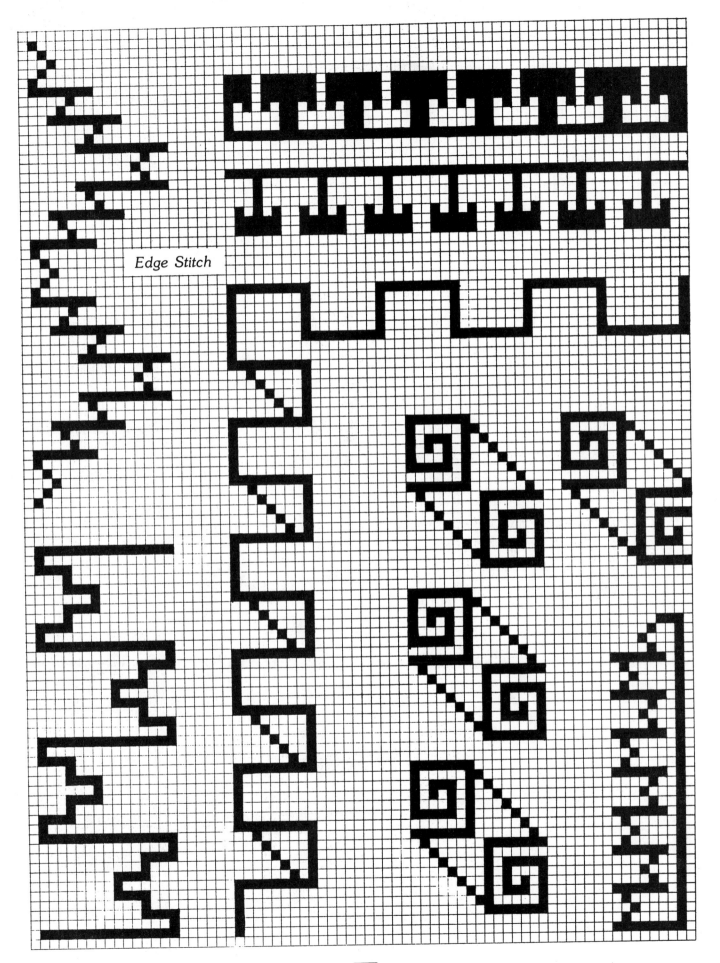

Edge Stitch

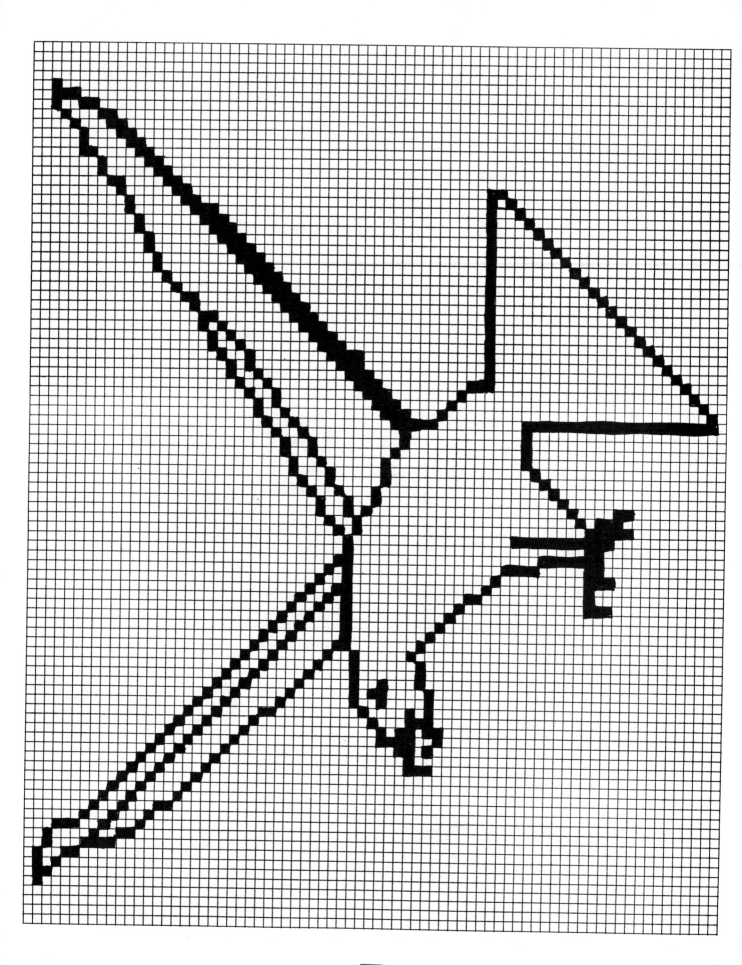

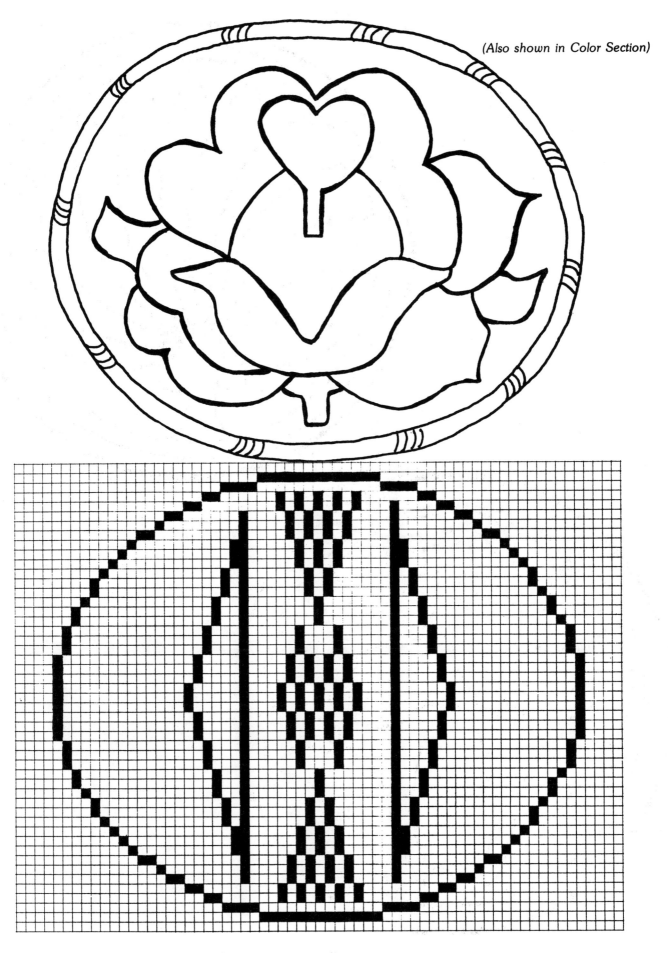

(Also shown in Color Section)

(Shown in Color Section)

Designs and Patterns
of the Plains Indian

Lazy Stitch Pattern

Applique
Stitch Patterns

94

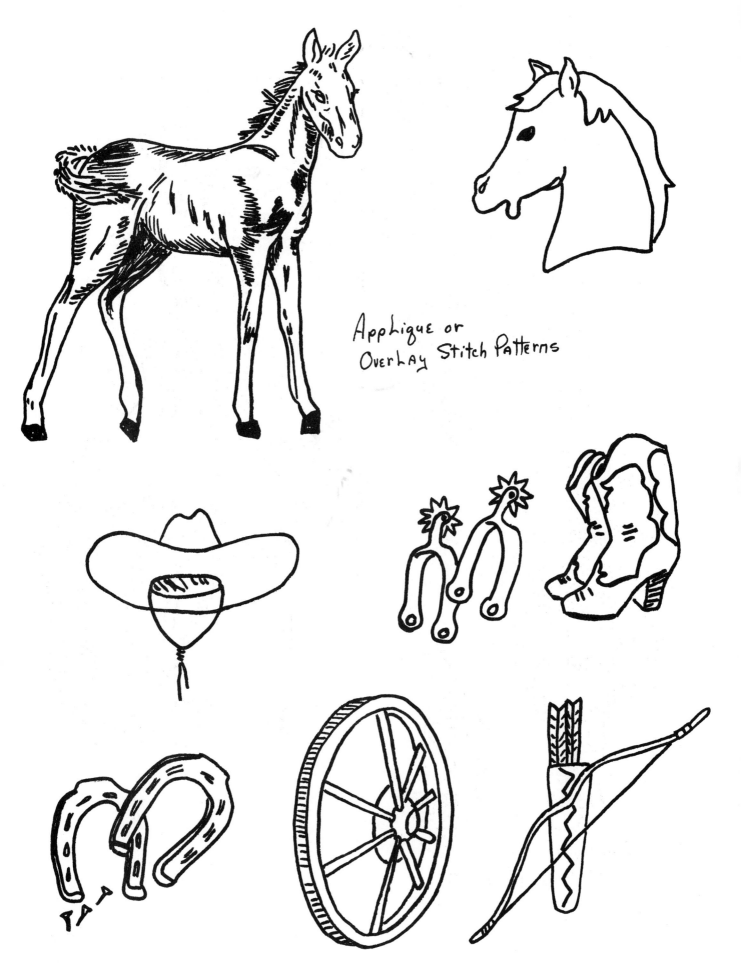

Applique or
Overlay Stitch Patterns